WAKE UP, SMELL THE MONEY

10 Steps to a Better Retirement Life

Pauline A Clarke

&

Kwame M.A. McPherson

WAKE UP, SMELL THE MONEY

10 Steps to a Better Retirement Life

Pauline A Clarke

&

Kwame M.A. McPherson

Disclaimer

The information contained in this book is for general information purposes only. The information is provided by PKM Group and while we endeavour to keep the information up to date and correct, we make no representations or warranties of any kind, express or implied, about the completeness, accuracy, reliability, suitability or availability with respect to this publication or the information, products, services, or related graphics contained in this publication for any purpose. Any reliance you place on such information is therefore strictly at your own risk.

In no event will we be liable for any loss or damage including without limitation, indirect or consequential loss or damage, or any loss or damage whatsoever arising from loss of data or profits arising out of, or in connection with, the use of this publication.

Through this publication you are able to link to other resources and contacts which are not under the control of PKM Group. We have no control over the nature, content and availability of those responsible for their management, operation or function. The inclusion of any links does not necessarily imply a recommendation or endorse the views expressed within them.

At the time of writing, every effort was made to keep the information in this publication current. However, PKM Group takes no responsibility for, and will not be liable for, information being out of date or unavailable due to technical or any other issue beyond our control.

PKM Group can be contacted at www.pkmi.co.uk

Copyright Year: August 2012, First edition

Copyright Notice: Published by PKM Group. All rights reserved. No part of this book may be reproduced in any form or by any means whatsoever, unless where permission is granted by PKM Group.

Results in this copyright notice:

© 2012 PKM Group. All rights reserved

ISBN: 978-1-291-11166-8

This book is dedicated to all those who are looking for a new way to enjoying a full life

CONTENTS

Acknowledgements — 9

Foreward — 11

Step 1 – The Time To Be Scared About Your Retirement Is Now! — 14

Step 2 – How Many Ways Do *You* Wish to Get Paid? — 18

Step 3 - What the Papers and Reports Say…what the future holds for *you* and *your* children? — 21

Step 4 – *Your* Retirement Timetable — 25

Step 5 - Pensions explained-what is a pension fund? — 33

Step 6 – Maximising Your Pension, SIPP or not SIPP? — 38

Step 7 - Retirement Abroad: *Qualified Non-UK Resident Pension Scheme (QNUPS)* — 43

Step 8 - Protecting *Your* Assets — 45

Step 9 - Making *Your* Money Work For *You*…in a recession or not! — 62

Step 10 - 7 Surefire Ways to Build *Your* Business and Make Your Money Work Harder — 65

***Your* Quality Life Checklist** — 82

Additional Resources and Contacts — 83

About the Authors — 85

Index 87

Acknowledgements

Raymond Aaron, NY Times Best Selling Author of *Double Your Income Doing What You Love*, for the inspiration and the phenomenal 10-10-10 program enabling us to complete this work in 10 weeks;

Our friends and families, enduring our work ethic and focus; the PKM Group for the inspiring platform to publish and motivate others;

Keith Williams, Future In Safe Hands, for his insight into the wider investment opportunities available to clients.

Louise Higham, LJ Financial Planning, ensuring their clients receive professional and candid advice;

The investment companies ensuring their clients receive more than favourable returns as well as security to protect the investment;

Stanley Taylor, JMD Associates, for the education on estate planning and trusts;

Shevonne Clarke, our editor, whose critical eye enabled this book to be better than it was.

Foreward

Retirement! The place we envisage we will get to someday after many years of work. Where we dream of putting our feet up, play golf, travel the world and watch our children and grandchildren forge their way in their own lives. Finally after years of toil, we now can rest, enjoying those golden years.

But with the accustomed lifestyle we acquired along the way, *will we be able to maintain it?* Especially with the rising cost of living each and every day, for example, a trolley full of groceries costs more today than it did just five years ago. The same can be said for utilities and every other consumable we use in our daily lives - everything has risen and continues to rise, so *how will* **we** *live? How will* **you** *live? What will* **you** *live on?*

For the majority of us, our retirement life will be financed from our pensions. *Question is - how many of us even know what a pension is much less what our retirement life looks like?*

The world of pensions can be a daunting complex place and difficult to maneuver thus trying to grasp its fundamentals and understand what it means for *you* can also be challenging. It can be grueling for the uneducated, from deciphering a complex pension statement to comprehending who the fund managers are managing and consistently realising profit from *your* depleting pension pot, year-on-year.

A recent article in the Daily Telegraph (*Annuity Crisis Sends Savers Reeling*, 1 September 2012) highlighted the dire straits which people are in currently and will eventually find themselves. It stated: "*Annuity rates continue to slide, piling on the agony for hundreds of thousands of new pensioners. Rates hit new lows this week, as Standard Life cut its annuity rates by 5pc, knocking £250 a year off the income from a £100,000 pension pot.* **The annuity crisis decimating the pensions of savers when they retire is set to continue for months, perhaps even years**."

As a result of this continuing and worrying urgency, *Wake Up, Smell the Money – 10 Steps to a Better Retirement Life* brings the complex world of pensions and what to do in preparation for retirement in easy, 'layman' terms to the average reader. This, in a way no other book has been able to achieve. The authors, Pauline Clarke and Kwame MA McPherson, based on their own personal experiences and after talking with the experts about pensions, decided to provide this book of invaluable education. The business partners and entrepreneurs felt a void needed to be filled, one where readers came away with important knowledge that empowered them into taking action.

A compelling and informative read, *Wake Up, Smell the Money – 10 Steps to a Better Retirement Life,* will provide you with the confidence and education you need in organising your retirement life today.

Raymond Aaron
NY Times Best Selling Author
www.UltimateAuthorBootcamp.com

Step 1 – The Time To Be Scared About Your Retirement Is Now!

Evening Standard, Wednesday May 28 2012, Page 45: *'Another reason why you can't retire, ever: The deficit of pension schemes in the FTSE 350 doubled in 2011 to £67 billion, says JLT Pension Capital Strategies. Keep working.'*

For the past decade, consecutive governments have warned of a pension crisis affecting each and every person contributing to a private or public pension fund.

According to the State of Retirement Report from LV= (once known as Liverpool Victoria), approximately 6.25 million people over the age of 50 will rely only on the state pension when they retire. Today, 1.25 million people live on state pension. As a result, it is predicted that many will not make any financial provision for their future retirement.

Ultimately, the government will not have the resources to care for those in retirement or those about to retire. This is the case for a couple of reasons. First, people are healthier and living longer. Second, employment as we know it has changed; employment is shrinking and unemployment is rising. Therefore, the taxation of a smaller pool of working people will be insufficient to maintain the pensions of those who are already retired and for the next generation to live their non-working lives[1].

As the economic woes continue, these are the questions you need to be asking yourself:

Where will I live?
Many people have invested in property as a potential retirement fund. Unfortunately, rising inflation, the expenses involved in keeping and maintaining a home, family disbursement - where children are either too busy to look after elders or have their own family to be concerned about - force many elderly people to sell their home just to maintain their care. Some end up in elderly care homes as a result of losing their home.

How will I pay for my bills?
According to The *Daily Express* (*Pay £100,000 For Old Age Care*, Saturday 24th March 2012), millions of taxpayers could be forced to pay £100,000 toward

---

[1] *'Another reason why you can't retire, ever: The deficit of pension schemes in the FTSE 350 doubled in 2011 to £67bn, says JLT Pension Capital Strategies. Keep working.'* Page 45, Evening Standard, Wednesday 23rd May 2012.

elderly care, and Chancellor George Osborne suggested that people would have to pay for their own care provision. As a result, it seemed probable that the savings threshold would rise from £35,000 to £100,000. The *Daily Mail* (*Frozen To Death As Fuel Bills Soar*, Monday 13th February 2012) highlighted that in the past five years, the number of pensioners dying from hypothermia had doubled due to cold winters and rises in energy bills.

What lifestyle plans do you have?

Are you certain you will be able to maintain your present lifestyle in the future? Think about that: when you retire you will no longer be in full or part-time employment, and you will need to continue to pay your bills, school fees and so on. Most significantly, inflation is also predicted to rise. How will you continue to pay for the same lifestyle in retirement?

Most importantly, what age do you want to retire? Will it be possible, or will you have to work till you drop?

It is calculated that we will all have to work until well into old age. How frightening is that?

Will you be able to support your family or will you need support from them?

Growing older will necessitate additional support. Will your children look after you or will you be able to look after yourself? Will you have the resources to do so? Will you need to rely on your children, thus losing your independence and burdening your children?

(This book will provide forward-thinking individuals with the tools to plan for a better financial future by exploring additional income streams, demystifying pensions, planning, and investment into tangible assets).

Step 2 – How Many Ways Do *You* Wish to Get Paid?

Daily Express, Tuesday May 1 2012, Headline: *'HOW MILLIONS MISS OUT ON BETTER PENSION: but there's an easy way to increase your income'*

In his book, *The Success Principles*[2], Jack Canfield states that the best way to enjoy income and develop economic security in your life is to create several sources of income. This will protect you in case any one of those sources – usually your job – dries up and leaves you without any cash flow.

Many people are unaware of how to create multiple streams of income.

What does that mean for the uninitiated?
Basically, it means having income coming from various channels. For example, you might have a profitable income-generating business or property investment. So we encourage potential clients to seek new income streams such as using *your* pension fund as an investment vehicle into income-generating, asset-rich products.

---

[2] Page 412, Chapter - Principle 60: To Spend More, First Make More

Revenue-producing assets vs negative investments

An investment (as described by the Oxford Dictionary), *is the action or process of investing money for profit*. The ability to make the right investment comes from learning and acquiring knowledge from those who have been successful in doing so.

So the most important thing to remember is: make profit-generating investments.

First impressions!

Many investments may look attractive but often do not guarantee the return of money invested, or the ROI (known as Return On Investment) seems high.

When considering any potential investments, it is best to **DO YOUR OWN DUE DILIGENCE**. This means educating yourself on how to make effective investment decisions. You can acquire your own Independent Financial Advisor (who will charge a fee) or specialist consultant within the industry. While the small print is often seen as a minefield securing professional advice can be seen as an expensive potential loss. Whichever your decision, it is critical to assess and understand the pros and cons of each opportunity. While no investments are risk-free, this approach ensures some security, and at least you have made an informed decision for yourself.

The media has been vocal about investment and future planning, so we will share some of the more relevant points with you.

Step 3 - What the Papers and Reports Say...what the future holds for *you* and *your* children?

Chris Salith's article in Money Marketing.com[3], **More Than One in Five Failing to Save for Retirement**, explains:

> More than one-fifth of people in the UK are failing to make any provision for their retirement, a survey by Scottish Widows found. The report covered 5,200 UK adults and found 22 per cent of people were not saving for retirement, up from 20 per cent in 2011. The Scottish Widows Pensions Index looked at those between 30 years-old and state pension age who earned more than £10,000 per year. It also found 54 per cent of adults polled were failing to save adequately for retirement, a record number up 5 per cent from 49 per cent in 2011.
>
> While retirement savings were falling, the report found people actually wanted a £200 increase in their annual pension income, from £24,300 in 2011 to £24,500 this year.

---

[3] 21 May 2012

The report said the average saver, calculated on a £25,000 salary and 8.9 per cent saving rate between age 30 and age 65, would receive around half this target if they retired at 65.

It stated the total pot for an average saver was around £150,000 in today's terms which would only provide an annual pension of £5,700. With the addition of the state pension this would generate a yearly income of approximately £13,000 which was well short of the £24,500 annual income people were looking for and would mean a total shortfall of £300,000. To meet current expectations, an average saver would need to save an additional £4,500 a year or £375 per month to make up the difference.

There's more....

Daily Mail, Friday February 17 2012, headlines: 'ONE IN 8 WOMEN WORKS PAST 70: and a tenth of men do the same'

The Telegraph.co.uk, November 13 2010: 'CLOCK TICKS DOWN ON PENSION DREAMS: Only a quarter of fiftysomething's are financially prepared for retirement, but there are steps you can take to catch up.'

Metro Newspaper, Thursday March 22 2012, headlines: 'TILL DEATH US DO WORK: children born today may have to wait until they are 80 before they can retire'

...And the Economy?

***Daily Express*, Wednesday August 31 2012, headline:** 'PENSION VALUES TO FALL BY 60%: workers told to save double for a comfortable retirement'

According to the learned economists, the global economy is suffering a breakdown and the national economy is performing poorly with little sign of recovery. David Kern, Chief Economist at the British Chambers of Commerce, says, *"Though growth will return, it will be over a longer period than expected. GDP and consumer spending will only return to pre-recession levels in the second half of 2014 or early in 2015. Though growth might be low, the economy will expand in spite of the difficulties continuing to face the Eurozone. However if there is a disorderly euro breakdown, then growth is likely to be lower."*

Step 4 – *Your* Retirement Timetable

Ok, so you're near that dreaded (or not) retirement age. After years of working, you finally see the finish line. You're considering where you can relax, travel or live your twilight years in comfort (or not).

Those who fail to plan for retirement could be in for a surprise when they realise the money they put away cannot sustain their current lifestyles and end up having to make major financial compromises. **So what do you do first?**

Successive governments have changed the goalposts for pensions, so there is no guarantee that what is currently paid out in pension benefit will exist in the years to come. **We encourage early planning.**

Whether age 20 or 55, we encourage everyone to plan for their future by exploring investment options that produce satisfying structured returns that will allow for a better, more comfortable retirement.

- **Find out what your pension plans are worth**

Before initiating a financial plan for the future, have an audit or a clear view of your current position. Identify both frozen and existing policies, especially if you have changed your address over the years; providers will not chase you or your estate to give you your money.

1. Establish your likely state pension entitlement (by completing Form BR19, available at www.direct.gov.uk).
2. Contact previous or current employees for details of their pension administrators who will then be able to provide you with your pension transfer values.
3. Contact the companies managing any private pension plans that you may have. Search online, but you may also have to write to them to confirm your position.
4. Call Pension Tracing (0845 600 2537) who will be able to cross-reference your national insurance number with plans you've registered.

5. Call the SERP hotline (0845 915 0150). This government department may be able to identify if you were eligible and where the funds were transferred. Otherwise known as S2P contributions.

All of this is *your* money, so monitor and manage it well. After all, your retirement is not a lottery!

- **How much money will you need?**

Examine how much income you will need to survive in retirement. Be realistic: don't forget to factor in holidays, gifts, cars, fees, subscriptions as well as mortgages, outstanding loans or any other debts that you may want to be cleared.

- **Seek advice on how to bridge the gap**

Chances are that what you are currently on target to receive is less than you'd ideally like. Seek advice about how you can bridge this gap. You need to maximize savings during this 10-year period, not only putting your money into pensions but also into other investments such as ISAs. Consider whether options such as retiring later or working part-time beyond your original planned retirement date may be a more realistic way of meeting your income retirement goals.

- **Review your investment strategy**

It is not only how much you save, but *where* it is invested that can make a difference. A spokesman for Origen, the pension's specialist, said: "Use this opportunity to carry out an audit of existing pension plans; look at where they are invested, how they have performed and what charges are levied on them. Don't forget to ask whether there are guarantees on any plans." Get advice about whether it makes sense to consolidate existing pension plans – perhaps via a SIPP (self-invested personal pension) – or take steps to protect capital values. There are a number of guaranteed products that can help you achieve this, but seek advice, as many come with higher charges.

As part of your review, look at the diversification of your assets, as this can help protect against sudden market movements. With a 10-year time frame, investors need to weigh up the risks of equity investments against safer cash-based products. Generally, the nearer to drawing your pension you are, the fewer investment risks you should take. But over this period it is reasonable to include equities within a mixed portfolio, particularly given the very low returns currently available on cash. Bonds, gilts and some structured products may provide a halfway house between cash and equities, but seek advice about costs and risks from a qualified IFA (Independent Financial Advisor).

- **Review retirement goals**

Get up-to-date pension forecasts and review your retirement plans. Is retiring at the age you planned still realistic and achievable? You can legally start your retirement at age 55, but it may be more appropriate to delay taking benefits in order to maximize fund growth.

- **Consider the safer option**

Consider moving stock market-based investments into safer options such as cash, bonds or gilts. If there is a sudden market correction now, you may have insufficient time to make good any losses.

- **Track 'lost' pensions**

If you've lost details of a pension scheme and need help contacting the provider, the Pension Tracing (0845 6002 537) may be able to help. It has access to information on over 200,000 schemes. The tracing service will use this database, free of charge, to search for your scheme and may be able to provide you with current contact details. Use this information to contact the pension provider and find out if you have any pension entitlement.

- **Maximize savings**

You now have just 60 pay packets left until you retire. Save what you can via pensions, ISAs and other investments. This, with your current pension pot, will have to produce enough for you to live off for 20 years. You may want to consider a pension for your spouse, which will dramatically reduce the money you will receive as part of the annuity plan. If you have maximized your pension contributions, it is also possible to contribute to a partner's pension plan.

Higher earners and those in final salary schemes should ensure any additional pension savings does not breach the lifetime allowance (£1.5m from April 2012) since this could land a tax bill. Those with outstanding debts, such as a mortgage or credit cards, could use spare cash to reduce or eliminate them.

- **Consider your retirement options**

Don't wait until the last minute to decide what you will do with your pension plan. Many people fail to consider their options properly and simply buy the annuity offered by their pension provider without further research. This can significantly reduce the income potential in retirement as there is no second opportunity to change to a better decision.

There are now many more retirement alternatives, including:
(1) Investment-linked,
(2) Flexible annuities,
(3) Phased retirement options,
(4) Conventional annuities and
(5) Income drawdown plans.
It is worth investigating which is most likely to suit your personal circumstances.

- **Seek annuity advice**

If you are buying an annuity, talk to an independent adviser about your options when it comes to shopping around for the best terms and rates. Remember that those who smoke or have health problems, even minor ones, should inform the annuity provider, as they are likely to get a better rate to reflect their reduced life expectancy.

- **Consider deferring retirement**

You may qualify for a larger pension if you defer taking benefits by a number of years. If you opt to do this, you need to contact the Pensions Service. Those who work beyond their retirement age do not have to make National Insurance contributions. Any additional money earned can still be saved in a pension plan and benefit from tax free growth.

- **Contact pension providers**

Establish the type of pension you have signed up for, ask when your pension will be paid, the value, the fees and transfer options. If you are deferring retirement, then they will need to be informed. You have the option of flexible planning, meaning you can cash in your fund and buy an annuity, transfer to a SIPP to ensure greater growth, or activate a pension drawdown.

Step 5 - Pensions explained-what is a pension fund?

The *Telegraph.co.uk*, Wednesday April 25 2012: *'OVER 50s WILL BE FORCED TO WORK 11 YEARS LONGER TO GET A DECENT PENSION: The Pensions Policy Institute warns that older workers aren't saving enough to secure a reasonable pension income.'*

The definition of a retirement or pension fund: A fund, from which pensions are paid, accumulated from contributions from employers, employees, or both.

The definition of pension: A regular payment made during a person's retirement from an investment fund to which that person or their employer has contributed.

A pension is often referred to as 'hidden money' since it is often overlooked until retirement but represents a significant way to efficiently create wealth tax.

Your own contributions to a private pension or your employer's company pension scheme play a critical part of your future financial security.

Get to know what you don't know.....

It is essential to understand how each of your pension plans works, what benefits you will receive, and when you can potentially look forward to retirement.

Familiarization with and monitoring of each fund and benefits should be a part of your planning process and should include the following:

1. What is the value of your fund?
    a. Protected rights (guaranteed)
    b. Unprotected rights (will be affected by stock market performance)
2. Where the fund is invested (EG: UK, international etc.)? What is the risk/exposure level?
3. What benefits are received by your estate if you have not bought an annuity or taken benefits?
4. What fees are payable on an annual basis?
5. Compare year on year to track real performance
6. Compare with the rate of inflation to assess real growth

So What Is An Annuity?

When you retire, the total value of your pension fund can buy an annuity, but you are allowed to take up to 25% of your pension fund as a tax-free lump sum straight away. The remaining 75% should be used to provide you with an income for your retirement life. Pension annuities are provided by the major insurance companies in the UK, who provide you with the rate they are prepared to pay based on your personal circumstances.

A *life annuity* or *lifetime immediate annuity* is used to provide an income in old age, such as a pension. Annuities offer another option for protection from creditors' claims. An annuity is an agreement whereby a person receives a sum of money regularly over a period of years. There are *fixed* annuities where the amounts are determined in the beginning, and *variable* annuities where the amount to be paid out depends upon the return on investment. To set one up, you can pay a lump sum, or you can make periodic payments. They are useful in asset protection planning because they are exempt from taxation.

Besides asset protection, another benefit available with annuities is the tax-free compounding of the investment, since the interest is not taxable until it is paid out.

If you live in a state that does not allow an exemption for annuities, there are annuities available outside the

UK, such as in Switzerland. Swiss law provides that if your beneficiary is your spouse or children, or made irrevocable, the annuity cannot be reached by creditors.

In order to guarantee that the income continues for life, the investment relies on cross-subsidy. Because an *annuity population* can be expected to have a distribution of lifespans around the population's average age, those dying earlier will support those living longer (longevity insurance). Cross-subsidy remains one of the most effective ways of spreading a given amount of capital and investment return over a lifetime without the risk of funds running out.

Cashing In Your Annuity

Traditionally you would cash your pension policy at a specific age (as detailed by your plan) by obtaining an annuity payment for life. Buying an annuity will give you approx. 3-5% of fund value (subject to your requirements) with no further fund growth. Try this calculator link:
http://www.find.co.uk/pensions/annuities_centre/annuities-calculator

Example: Without spousal benefits, a £100,000 fund will guarantee £6,034 per annum, guaranteed for 10 years via Aviva. The graph below indicates annuity trends since July 2007.[4]

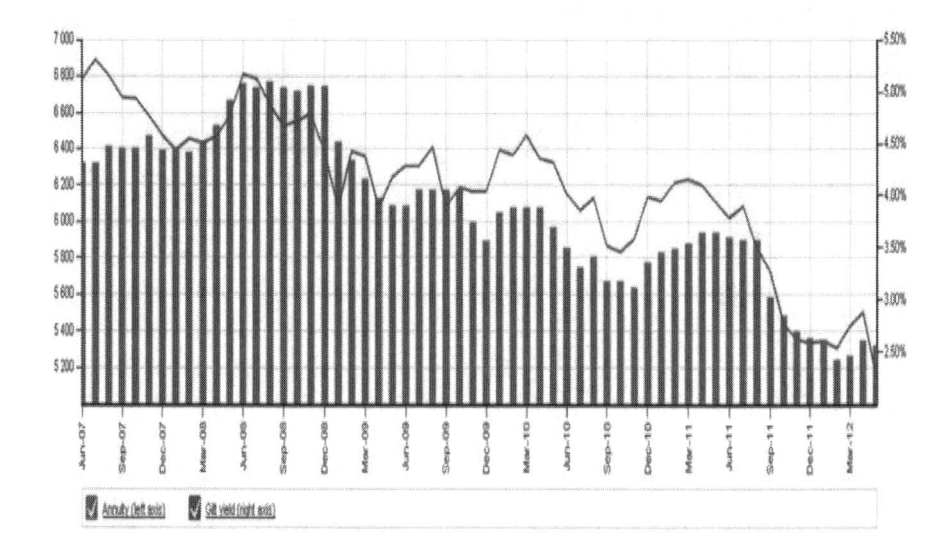

¹ Male age 65, Female 60, £100,000 purchase, joint life 2/3rds, guaranteed 5 years and level payments

---

[4] Source: Annuities Online, http://www.annuities-online.com/rates/AnnuityRates.aspx is a very useful link regarding rates and pros and cons of draw down.

Step 6 – Maximising Your Pension, SIPP or not SIPP?

To SIPP or not to SIPP: defining a Self-Invested Personal Pension (SIPP)

A SIPP, as it is commonly known, is the <u>name given to personal pension schemes, UK government approved, which are managed by individuals who make their own investment decisions. These investment vehicles have to be approved by HM Revenue & Customs (HMRC)</u>.

A SIPP is a pension bank account (investment wrapper) administered by a third party and approved by the Financial Services Authority and HMRC, but managed by you in terms of the types of investments, timescales for exit, drawing benefits or buying an annuity.

A SIPP can provide you with the option of 'Income Draw Down' (suitable for funds of £80k+) representing approx 7% pa. However, SIPPs have the flexibility to enjoy fund growth through asset returns representing between 6-15% p.a., thus providing the liquidity needed for the draw down.

As with any investment portfolio, it is recommended an individual consider a spread of asset-based investments as opposed to stocks and shares that have lately been quite volatile, with limited growth.

On death, if you have not drawn benefits from the SIPP, then 100% of the value will be transferred to your estate outside of Inheritance Tax Allowance.

If benefits are drawn it is then subject to tax.

A number of funds can be transferred into a SIPP for greater investment development over 5-10 years, which will also achieve a better annuity rate. Transferring funds can also provide income draw down for benefits on the total fund whilst still generating interest from existing assets within the portfolio.

Standard versus Alternative Investments

Whilst the stock markets have not performed well, the opportunity to improve returns can be met with Alternative Investments.

Alternative investments are generally not regulated by the FSA, so they're not protected under the compensation scheme which would look to return up to 80% of your initial investment. However, all organisations have to go through rigorous procedures to gain approval for SIPP pension investment from the HMRC.

Benefits of Alternative Investments

Alternative investments:
- Diversify an investor's portfolio.
- Reduce risks.
- Offer good profit generating opportunities.
- Direct control.
- Direct agreement often with contractual returns and defined exit strategies.

Drawbacks of Alternative Investments

The limitations of alternative investments are:
- The liquidity of these investments is lower than that of stocks, bonds and cash.
- These investments require specific expertise, as a result of which the costs associated with due diligence are high.
- It is difficult to establish benchmarks for these investments. This hinders the performance

appraisal of the investments. Moreover, the limited availability of performance data impacts an investor's ability to make an informed choice.

Examples of Alternative Investments

Exposure to these limited investment options raises the risk profile. Portfolio diversification, or holding assets with different characteristics, is an effective way of reducing the risk exposure for the same level of profit potential which can be achieved through alternative investments. Investments made into assets that do not fall under one of the three traditional asset types (cash, stocks and bonds) are called alternative investments.

Alternative Investments: Types

Alternate investments usually require a minimum fixed capital lump sum. The most common alternative investments are:

- Real estate. This investment option involves buying and selling immovable property, such as land and buildings. This investment yields rental income as well as capital appreciation in some cases. Hotel developments, which occasionally do not require any maintenance fees or associated costs, can also be included.

- Commercial Land. Often on a long lease, land is used to grow crops or timber, which is the source of ROI income. Check on this type of investment and explore exit strategies, as some investment forecasts appear to be excessive.
- Art. The financial crisis of 2008 saw a prolonged downturn in the stock market, a slowdown in the economy and low interest rates. Shortly after, the popularity of art as an alternative investment rose significantly.
- Gold and precious metals. Gold is a defensive investment and becomes more popular during periods of prolonged economic and political upheavals.
- Wine. Investments in fine wine have yielded healthy returns over the past few years. Wine investments also remained relatively insulated from the 2007-2008 credit crunch.

We hope you have gained valuable information that you can share with others, because ignorance isn't bliss, just very expensive.

Step 7 - Retirement Abroad: *Qualified Non-UK Resident Pension Scheme (QNUPS)*

QNUPS (Qualified Non-UK Pension Schemes) are a form of overseas pensions available to both those who are U.K. domiciled (whether U.K. resident or not) and are seeking to move overseas in retirement.

QNUPS are most commonly used by ex-pats who are planning on retiring outside the U.K., and therefore have the potential to get a preferential tax rate in the country they are retiring in as well as alleviate U.K. inheritance tax (IHT). However, you do not need to be planning to retire abroad to be eligible; they are available to anyone who is U.K. domiciled (whether a U.K. resident or not). In February 2010, the Government introduced Qualifying Non–UK Pension Schemes (QNUPS) to correct an uncertainty around previous legislation. Its aim was to exempt a pension fund from Inheritance Tax on the death of a pension member if no lump sum or other payment was drawn down from the retirement fund.

QNUPS benefits

Assets are effectively removed from the U.K. tax net and introduced to a new tax environment depending on expat's residence, leading to a substantial increase in income derived from the retirement fund. QNUPS also allows individuals to invest more regularly into their pension pot than the UK annual allowance of £50,000.

The downside is that you will not be able to return to the U.K. for social benefits.

Step 8 - Protecting *Your* Assets

Without proper protection, the assets that you have worked long and hard to accumulate can be lost within a very short period if you are sued, file for bankruptcy, or you are otherwise subject to judgements proceedings. However, understanding that certain assets should be protected from being lost in such circumstances, lawmakers have passed acts under which certain types of assets are, or can be, shielded. If you become unable to look after yourself due to illness or accident, the state will step in and charge you unless you have appointed someone to act on your behalf in the form of a lasting power of attorney[5].

In this article, we'll show you what measures you can take to protect your savings.

Everyone with Assets is at Risk

You may think that only doctors, corporate executives and others in litigation-prone professions are the only ones who need to worry about protecting their assets. Not so. There are many circumstances under which

---

[5] *What is a Lasting Power of Attorney?* It is a legal document enabling someone to appoint one or more people to manage their affairs should they become mentally incapable of doing so themselves.

your assets can be attached or garnished, including filing for bankruptcy, getting a divorce, or being on the defensive end of a civil lawsuit. Most people don't even consider many of these circumstances until they occur. For instance, if your teenage child is on the wrongful end of a motor car accident, that could result in the damaged party going after your assets.

Some of the common methods for asset protection include:

Asset Protection Trusts
For years, wealthy individuals have used offshore trusts in such locations as the Cook Islands and Nevis to protect assets from creditors. While you don't even have to be a resident of the country to buy into one of these trusts, they can be expensive to establish and maintain, so we suggest you seek professional advice if you are considering establishing one.

Asset protection trusts offer a way to transfer a portion of your assets into a trust run by an independent trustee. The trust's assets will be out of the reach of most creditors, and you can receive occasional distributions. These trusts may even allow you to shield the assets for your children when they are mature enough to manage them.

The requirements for an asset protection trust include the following:

- It must be irrevocable.
- It must have an independent trustee that is an individual located in the state or is a bank and trust company.
- It must only allow distributions at the trustee's discretion.
- It must have a spendthrift clause.
- Some or all of the trust's assets must be located in the trust's state.
- The trust's documents and administration must be in the state.
- If you are considering looking into an asset protection trust, be sure to work with an attorney who is experienced and proficient in this field. Many individuals have run afoul of tax laws because their trusts did not satisfy regulatory requirements.

Accounts-Receivable Financing

If you own a business, you could borrow against its receivables and put the money into a non-business account. This would make the debt-encumbered asset less attractive to your creditors, and make otherwise reachable assets unreachable by creditors.

Strip Out Your Equity

One option for protecting your assets is to pull the equity out of them and put that cash into assets. For example, suppose you own a commercial building and are concerned about potential lawsuits. If you took out a loan against the building's equity, you could place the funds in a protected asset, such as an annuity.

Family Limited Partnerships

Assets transferred into a family limited partnership (FLP) are exchanged for shares in the partnership. Because the FLP owns the assets, they are protected from creditors under the Uniform Limited Partnership Act. However, you control the FLP and, thus, the assets. There is no market for the shares you receive, so their value is significantly less than the value of the asset exchanged.

Less Complex Ways to Protect Assets

There are some inexpensive, simple ways to protect assets that anyone can implement:

- You could transfer assets to your spouse's name. However, if you divorce, the end results could be different from what you intended.
- Put more money into your employer-contribution pension plan because it might have unlimited protection.
- Buy an insurance policy that protects you from personal-injury, redundancy (income protection) as well as critical illness above the standard coverage offered in your home and car policies.
- Make the most of UK laws covering taxes, annuities and life insurance. For instance, paying down your mortgage could protect cash that is otherwise vulnerable.
- Don't mix business assets with personal assets. That way, if your company runs into a problem, your personal assets might not be at risk and vice versa.

Some Final Words of Caution

You may have seen self-proclaimed asset-protection experts advertise their seminars or easy-to-use kits on TV or the internet. Before deciding to use any of these services, you should perform extensive research, including checking with the Better Business Bureau. And before you take any of the steps discussed in this book, meet with a solicitor or specialist who is familiar with the law and an expert in the asset protection field. Most importantly, don't wait until you have a judgment against you. By then it may be too late, and the courts could declare that you made a "fraudulent transfer" to get out of meeting your obligations.

A Life Plan for Your Assets

Life insurance and annuities may be used for asset protection as well as estate planning. U.K. laws include certain exemptions: for the cash value or the proceeds of life insurance, for wages and for your home. With annuities the law protects them from creditors, though some do vary in terms of the amount protected and under what circumstances they are protected.

- **Life Insurance**

There are two basic types of life insurance: term life, in which you pay only for a death benefit, and whole life, in which you pay additional money, which builds up as savings. Upon your death, the proceeds can pass to your beneficiaries free of any claims by your creditors. In some cases, property that is purchased with the proceeds of a life insurance policy is also exempt.

However, there are exceptions to this protection; a life insurance policy is only exempt from creditors' claims if the beneficiaries are the spouse, children or other dependents. If the owner of the policy has the power to change the beneficiary, the proceeds are not protected. Additionally, even if a policy is originally exempt, the protection can be lost by:

- Assigning your policy to a creditor. Note that loan papers prepared by banks often contain clauses that can give the bank a right to your life insurance policy. Read the fine print!
- Buying a policy and paying the premium for it when you are insolvent. This would constitute a fraudulent conveyance and, if challenged, could be found non-exempt.
- Changing the beneficiary while you are insolvent.

If another person owns your insurance policy, your creditors cannot reach it because it is not your property. If you make a gift of your policy to your spouse or children, the gift must be absolute. You may not retain any control over the policy or you will lose the asset protection benefit.

Extra asset protection may be provided if you place your insurance policy in an irrevocable life insurance trust. With this type of trust, you transfer either an existing policy or the funds to buy one.

- **In death**

    "Three things are guaranteed in life: Death, Old Clothes and Taxation" – *We will outline some planning options for Death and Taxation!*

Death insurance is more commonly referred to as life insurance. It is insurance that provides a cash benefit to survivors upon the death of the insured person. Choosing life insurance can be confusing, as there are many different types and features available. Life insurance can be used for whatever purposes the beneficiary sees fit, EG: to cover funeral costs (which can be very expensive when a basic ceremony in the U.K. averages £3,300, excluding any hospitality). Detail your exact wishes to your nearest and dearest.

- **Significance**

Surviving spouses and children of adults who die without any kind of life insurance can be hit hard by both the costs of final expenses and the loss of income. Internationally, studies indicate that fully 40 percent of the adult population has absolutely no life insurance. Of those who are insured, it is estimated that most policies are inadequate, which forces the surviving spouse to make drastic lifestyle changes to stay current with the family's financial obligations. This can force the family to change residences or sell possessions.

- **Function**

In the past, life insurance was called "death insurance" because its primary function was thought to be simply to pay for funeral expenses. Now, however, life insurance has become important in helping the surviving family members maintain their regular lifestyle and place of residence. This is particularly important if one spouse is a stay-at-home parent or may not be prepared to immediately enter the workforce after the death of his or her partner. In the case of cash value life insurance, it can also be used as a form of investment and turned in for cash at a later date.

- **Types**

There are two primary types of life insurance: *term* life insurance and *whole* life insurance. Both types of insurance pay a lump sum of money to the beneficiary upon the death of the policy holder. Term life is the least expensive insurance option, as it accrues no cash value. With a term policy, the premiums (the amount paid for the policy) are locked in only for a specific amount of time, after which the rates for renewal can be higher. By contrast, whole life insurance is more expensive, but builds cash value over time. The premiums for a whole life policy remain the same throughout the lifetime of the insured, provided that he maintains coverage.

- **Considerations**

Determining how much life insurance to buy can be difficult. An insurance website explains that although there are many different methods of calculating how much life insurance a family needs, the best way to get adequate insurance is to sit down with a qualified agent and discuss your family's finances in depth. He can help you choose the proper benefit amount for all adults in your household. Ideally, there should be enough money for the family to pay off any existing mortgage and debt, as well as providing the amount that the deceased's income contributed for a period of two years. This amount will generally fall somewhere between six and 10 time the insured's gross yearly salary.

- **Insight**

Here's a tip for getting the most out of your life-insurance premium. You can avoid a common mistake made by many consumers by buying more than one policy *per person*. For example, you can purchase a policy as part of an employee benefit package and then buy additional individual insurance. Because each policy has some fees attached, the price of two policies that add up to £100,000 will be more than that of one policy worth the same amount. The most efficient way to find the best life-insurance policy is to go to a reliable insurance comparison website. As long as the company is financially stable, there is very little difference from policy to policy. However, rates between different companies can vary greatly, so it pays to shop around.

- **Estate Planning**

Estate planning is an ongoing process and should be started as soon as one has any measurable asset base. As life progresses and goals shift, the estate plan should be modified to align with new goals. Lack of adequate estate planning can cause undue financial burdens to loved ones (inheritance tax can run higher than 40%), so at the very least a **Will** should be set up even if the taxable estate is not large.

- **Wills**

A Will is the easiest and cheapest estate planning document to prepare. Most people can create their own will without hiring a solicitor (with a DIY pack or by going online), but be cautious. After you are gone, your will must be probated, so we would suggest doing it properly to avoid any confusion. Probate is a process whereby your loved ones must adhere to the division of your estate in accordance with your wishes.

Because of the complexity of the probate process, it is almost impossible for a family to probate a will without hiring a solicitor to execute any legal transfer of your assets.

Be sure to appoint your own executor, or possibly two, to coordinate your affairs with prior notification, along with assembling your paperwork where it can be found.

Beware of appointing your bank, which is likely to take a considerable percentage in addition to costs and may not necessarily be focused on processing (as it not their core business).

Prior to committing, get confirmation of all costs associated with the writing, storage and execution, and shop around for the best deals.

- **The Document for Young Families**

A will may be the document of choice for a young family for several reasons. First, a will is the only document that allows you to name a guardian for your minor children. It is not necessary to name a guardian if there is a natural parent living. However, if both natural parents are gone, a will gives you the opportunity to choose the person or persons you would like to raise your children.

If you do not have a will, and both natural parents are gone, the courts will conduct hearings to determine who should serve as the legal guardian of your minor children. A person who petitions the court to serve as legal guardian may not be the person you would have chosen had you prepared for this eventuality in advance. If this thought scares you, keep in mind that it is very difficult for someone to contest your choice of a guardian when you name that person in your will.

The second reason a young person or family might choose to have a will rather than other legal arrangements is because a will is easy and inexpensive to prepare and amend. A young person is less likely to die than someone older, but even in the unlikely event of a premature death, it is important that your instructions be contained in a legally binding document.

- **Uncomplicated Affairs**

If you are older and your affairs are not complex, you may still choose to have a will to ensure that your property passes to the loved ones of your choice.

Although there may be some costs in distributing your assets when you are gone, a will is an excellent estate planning document.

- **Trust**

A trust is an agreement that describes how assets will be managed and held for the benefit of another person. There are many types of trusts, designed for different purposes, so let's begin discussing the elements common to most types of trusts (and for related reading, check out *Pick The Perfect Trust*[6]).

Trust Classifications

Trusts can have the following types of classifications:

> *Living Trust*
> A living trust is usually created by the grantor during his or her lifetime through a transfer of property to a trustee. The grantor generally retains the power to change or revoke the trust. When the grantor passes away, this trust becomes irrevocable, which means that the terms of the trust cannot be changed, and the trustee must follow the rules set forth in the trust concerning the distribution of property and the payment of taxes and expenses.

---

[6] *www.investopedia.com/articles/pf/08/trust-basics.asp*

Testamentary Trust

Testamentary Trust, sometimes called trusts under will are trusts that are created by a will after the grantor dies. This type of trust is designed to accomplish specific planning goals, such as:

- Preserving assets for children from a previous marriage.
- Protecting a spouse's financial future by providing lifetime income, available under a qualified terminable interest property (QTIP) trust.
- Skipping the surviving spouse entirely as a beneficiary.
- Ensuring that a special-needs beneficiary will be taken care of.
- Preventing minors from inheriting property outright when they reach the age or majority as defined by the law - usually from age 18 – 21, or 30 in the case of Prince William.
- Gifting to charities.

Funded

A trust may be fully or partially funded by the grantor during his or her lifetime or after death.

In the case of a funded trust, it means that property has been put inside the trust.

Unfunded

An unfunded trust is simply the trust agreement. Some trusts remain unfunded until the death of the grantor, or may just stay unfunded.

Revocable

A revocable trust (also called "modifiable") can be changed by the grantor during his or her lifetime.

Irrevocable

By contrast, an irrevocable trust (also called "non-modifiable") cannot be changed by the grantor once the trust is deemed irrevocable. The grantor loses total control of the property and has to obey the trust rules. A trust can be revocable during the grantor's lifetime and becomes irrevocable upon death.

Goals of Trusts

There are many reasons why you may choose to have a trust as part of your estate plan, including avoiding probate, providing financial support to family members and gaining privacy advantages if the state where you live requires filing an inventory of assets.

- **In Sickness**

Whilst we have a way of planning for death, preparation is not generally considered for sickness, when you may be unable to make decisions for yourself and manage your life. The reality is that if you are single, then (in extreme cases) the government has the right to manage your estate, organize your children and sell your house to pay your way until such time that you die or recover. There is a strong possibility of excessive charges that you will not be able to challenge.

The only option to manage this eventuality is to set up a "Lasting Power of Attorney," which will indicate who you want to carry out your wishes in terms of managing your estate and bills.

Step 9 - Making *Your* Money Work For *You*...in a recession or not!

When it comes to saving and making money, you should assess all areas of your life. You can trim your personal budget, complete training to improve your skills, and re-evaluate direct or pension investments or other income streams. Today's economy has forced many to seek new revenue and in making the transition from only having or looking at a single income stream, a process of education *needs* to take place. This includes reading books about creating wealth, attending seminars and workshops with a focus on empowerment, re-training for new skills and opportunities and about investing. But most importantly, it's about you taking ACTION.

So what follows is an overview of the options available to you to make a difference right away.

Revenue Streams using the internet:

- **Direct**

Direct revenue is revenue earned from pre-paid advertisements and sponsorships shown on websites. At the end of each month, we compute how much each of our direct revenue advertisements earned per page view, and share 20% of that revenue with all of our active affiliates.

- **Indirect**

Indirect revenue is revenue earned through external affiliate programs in which we participate, and which is paid periodically to us. Because of the time lag between when indirect revenue is earned, and when the revenue is received, it is not possible to track that revenue back to specific pages shown to visitors sent to us by our affiliates. We share 20% of our indirect revenue with all affiliates who are active in the month that we actually receive that revenue.

- **Referral**

The business of referrals makes sense for most companies for the following reasons:
- Referral marketing reduces your sales expenses and sales cycle. With less time spent cold calling prospects, your small business can focus on customers and their circles of influence.
- Referrals can build your base of satisfied customers. The cycle self-perpetuates with more satisfied customers referring others to your company.

- Referrals increase your sales revenue. According to world-renowned sales trainer Tom Hopkins, in "Sales Prospecting for Dummies," your closing ratio for non-qualified leads is 10 percent versus a 60 percent close ratio with referred leads.

If the prospect of building the referral end of your business is so enticing, why do so few businesses do it? Because they use the wrong approach in building referrals and have limited success. To ensure your business is on track to building referrals, follow **Step 10**.

Step 10 - 7 Surefire Ways to Build *Your* Business and Make Your Money Work Harder

1. Set A Target. In business, measure the results to improve performance. Set a clear goal with a time line. For Example, you could aim for a 10% increase in referral business over the next 10 weeks.

2. Timing. Conventional sales wisdom claims the best time to ask for the referral is immediately after the close. This tactic is far too aggressive. Give your clients time to experience your service or product before asking for a referral. Ask for the referral at close only if your client is already delighted with your business.

3. Top 20. Not all customers are referral candidates. Find the top 20% that are ecstatic about your business and ask them for referrals. Make sure their network is the type of client you want.

4. Give and You'll Receive. Give your clients extra service and follow-up support before asking for

referrals. When you give willingly to your customers, they will return the favour.

5. Type of Customer. Inform your referring clients of the type of customers you can help. Providing a clear picture of the customer demographics will help your referral marketing.

6. Rewards Program. Provide special rewards to your referring customers on a regular basis. If a customer provides you with 5 sales, offer them something special, e.g. discounts or major value extras.

7. Thank-You. Lisa A. Maini, President of My Marketing Manager, recommends that businesses establish trust to build referrals. Maini says, "Create a basic thank you letter that can be personalized and sent to each referral you receive. Treat your referral sources with the utmost of care and you will not only build a foundation of trust but keep hot prospects coming to your door."

Multilevel Marketing

There are three types of multi-level marketing (MLM - also known as Networking Marketing) businesses based on their major source of revenue: those that sell a product, those that sell a service, and those that sell memberships. MLM businesses are made attractive to potential salespeople because they can earn commissions not only from the sale of the goods or services they sell themselves, but also from the sales of those they recruit into the business. While many MLMs are very reputable and successful businesses, some have employed questionable marketing and recruiting tactics, sullying the reputation of the entire industry.

MLM businesses are generally regular businesses selling products or services. Multi-level marketing is their approach to distribution and sales; instead of selling goods out of a storefront or services from an office, they contract with individuals to do their selling as independent contractors. Variously titled associates, distributors, representatives, or affiliates, they reach out to potential customers in a number of different ways, including traditional advertising, online approaches, and door-to-door direct sales. New associates typically pay significant fees to join the sales force, and are sometimes permitted to advance to managerial status for a higher fee.

MLM associates earn commissions on their own sales, and they earn smaller commissions, or overrides, on the sales of those associates they've recruited to the business. When an associate recruits a new associate, that new associate becomes part of the recruiter's "downline," which comprises all an associate's recruits, plus all of their recruits. Most MLM compensation packages offer overrides on second-, third-, and fourth-generation recruits, and some offer overrides on an associate's entire downline.

MLM businesses that sell products usually make the product themselves, but in some cases, they'll contract with a third party to manufacture it with the MLM's label. Examples of such products include vitamins and nutritional supplements, cosmetics and beauty aids, cleaning supplies and other household products, and other products that lend themselves to impulse and repeat purchases. While some associates will maintain an inventory of the product for immediate delivery when a sale is made, most take orders and transmit them to the home office. Some companies' ship orders directly to the customers; others deliver orders in bulk to the associates, who then hand-deliver them to the customers. In either case, associates' compensation is based on the dollar value of products ordered and paid for.

MLM businesses that sell services, on the other hand, have no need for inventories or recurring visits to clients. Their associates market the company's services the same way as the product-selling associates, and are compensated similarly. Instead of selling a product, though, they sell memberships to the company's service. There's very little commission paid for renewal memberships, however, so an associate must constantly find new clients to maintain a good income. Service-oriented MLMs sell online education plans, club memberships, legal services, financial services, and similar services.

The third type of MLM business sells memberships, and can more accurately be classified as a pyramid scheme. These MLMs concentrate on recruiting new associates, and there's little attention paid to selling a product or service. These MLM businesses pay associates a significant commission for recruiting new associates, providing an added incentive to seek revenue from a source other than the company's product or service. Without an emphasis on earning revenue from the sale of a service or product, such MLM businesses inevitably collapse.

Many MLM businesses are very successful. Despite their success, however, most research indicates that the majority of associates don't earn enough from commissions and overrides even to pay their expenses. The companies, on the other hand, earn money not only from the sales of the products or services, but also from the sign-up fees charged to new associates. Many MLMs also sell their associates a wide range of sales support materials, such as presentation binders and other promotional material, and even require that business cards and other stationery items be ordered through the company.

The success of some of the large MLM businesses has led to a wide range of imitators. Some of these imitators' activities have prompted investigations, which have cast a shadow on the entire industry. Those considering joining an MLM should carefully perform their own due diligence before signing any agreement or paying any fees. Examples include: Avon, Amway and so on.

Investment Business Opportunities

It takes money to make money. Once you have a little bit of capital, you can do the wise thing and invest it in a business to try and make your money grow. Unfortunately, the challenges are as large as the rewards, and investing usually isn't as easy as simply writing a check. In order to make a wise investment in a business, you need to invest more than just your money. After all, you're becoming a part-owner in the business. Here's how to invest in a business and, hopefully, make money.

| Investing, what that? | When you put money somewhere and gain interest and growth. | So why do I need to make a pension investment? | If you want to be poor in retirement, don't take control. | Hm...why do I need to take your word? | When last did you pay for a drink? |

Investment Planning

1. Consider supply and demand. Does the company produce a product or provide a service that people will need? If it's a regional business, is there enough of a market for what the business is selling? Be honest with yourself; it's easy to get wrapped up when it comes to a big opportunity.

2. Finish your research by looking toward the future. Representatives of the business in which you're interested will provide you with all kinds of projections about what they expect the company to make over the next few years. Do these make sense? They're using educated guesses to predict future revenues. A lot can go wrong and a lot of things can change, so decide if the company's representatives are providing enough room for error.

3. Consult an investment professional. If you're investing in a large, public business, you can speak with a broker to confirm or refute your suspicions about the business. The broker can also serve as the middleman between you and the business in which you're investing.

4. Deal directly with the officers of the business. This can be a lot of fun, especially if you're getting in on the ground floor of a new company. It's exciting knowing you're a part of a new venture that could change the world (or at least provide a nice cushion, holiday or pay your child's tuition). Dealing with the owners of an established business

is a different kind of fun, as some of the risk is reduced.

5. Purchase stocks and shares to invest in a business. While you'll have less influence on day-to-day operations, you'll still own a little part of it. There are A, B and C class options for shares, and some allow you to vote on big decisions at stockholder meetings while others do not. Consider which shares will pay the highest dividends, giving you an additional source of income.

Investment Areas

It really is nearly a rhetorical question. Investing is the best way to secure your future. In this world there are two ways to earn income: exchange your labour for cash, or have your money earn money for you. The rich do the latter and the poor don't. It's as simple as that.

Money kept in a "savings" account is earning interest at rates that don't even keep pace with inflation, so you need to find the best place to put your money to beat inflation by a substantial amount. Average interest rates on savings accounts are currently less than 2%.

Below are a range of investment references you may have seen in the media, so we've included them for your consideration.

- Futures. These are standardised contracts for the sale and purchase of a commodity on a specified date and at a predetermined price. Futures can be used to trade currencies and commodities (such as oil and agricultural products). People can also invest in S&P and NASDAQ futures.
- Options. These are similar to futures. The only difference is that the holder of an options contract is under no obligation to buy or sell the underlying asset. S/he can just let the contract expire.
- ETFs. Exchange traded funds (ETFs) hold assets such as stocks, bonds, commodities and precious metals. These ETFs are traded on the stock exchange at a price that equals the net asset value (NAV) of the underlying asset. The most common ETFs used as alternative investments are gold and oil.
- Hedged funds. These funds invest in a broad range of investment options including stocks, debt and commodities. They often aim at offsetting potential losses in the markets they invest in. They use

methods like short selling to hedge their investments.
- Establish where you can find investments that will serve your needs.

There is always risk in anything you do, but with education and research you can minimise that risk. As you get more education you can better decide how much risk you want to take, and conversely, how much return you need to make. Understanding the risks is the first step toward minimizing them. In fact, it is possible to make 10-15% annual return on your investment with almost no risk, if you know what you are doing.

One strategy that investors have been using for years is that of diversification. You do this by having investments in a range of different companies from blue chips to tech stocks, while also having some investments in bonds. To get a nice range of stocks some people use mutual funds to spread their investments without having to do a lot of research on different companies. This gives you diversification, and also has a professional taking care of the research end of that part of your investment portfolio.

While there are many paths you can go down when you get into investing in the stock market, there's one thing you can be sure of: with education and research you will make money. You are already beginning your education here, and that's a great start. Continue on this road and make your money work for you.

Pension Investments

It's true that people retiring in 2012 will be far less affluent than they were in 1980. Accordingly, you'll want to make sure your pension is poised to produce the best possible return. But deciding how to invest your pension is far from a simple task, so here are the key factors you will need to consider.

But let's look at the basics first. When you open a pension plan you'll be asked where you want your money invested and you'll usually be expected to select from a range of investment funds presented. A fund is simply a pooled investment which combines money from thousands of individual investors which is then invested on their behalf by a fund manager.

If you don't make a selection, your money will usually be invested in the scheme's 'default' fund. But that's unlikely to be the best choice for you. When it comes to pensions, one size certainly does not fit all!

So it pays to consider your investment options more carefully. But how do you know which funds are a good choice? Well, that largely depends on how old you are your attitude toward risk and your investment objectives.

Most funds invest in one or more of the four major asset classes: cash, fixed-interest bonds, property and shares. Let's look at each of these in turn. First up....

Cash

Cash is the least risky asset class because the capital you invest is guaranteed with interest earned on top. However, your capital is at risk from the effects of inflation (rising prices) and an interest rate which could fall.

Because cash is a safe bet, don't expect a phenomenal rate of return. Generally, the lower the risk you take, the lower the return. But if you're within say, 10 years of retiring, it's a good idea to move some of your pension out of higher-risk assets and into cash to protect its value before you take the benefits.

ISAs

ISAs are a very tax-efficient way to save with a maximum limit set each year as to how much you can invest. Many ISA vehicles will promote an interest rate of 3%+, but terms may dictate that the funds must stay in the account for a fixed period. Watch the small print, since interest bonuses may be paid on the anniversary and penalties may be incurred if terms are not adhered to. More importantly, you need to watch what the interest rate drops to after the promotional period. Take advantage of transferring your accumulated ISA fund around to maximise investment growth.

Fixed Interest Bonds

A bond is essentially a loan to a bond issuer. In other words, you're lending money to the bond issuer who pays you a fixed rate of interest in return. There are two main types: gilts and corporate bonds. Gilts are issued by the government while corporate bonds are issued by companies.

Bonds are deemed to be lower risk because there's some security provided by the fixed interest rate. But again, the potential for growth is restricted. As with cash, older investors approaching retirement may wish to move some of their pension fund into bonds to help preserve its value.

Property

In the context of pensions, this relates to commercial property such as offices and retail space, not residential housing. Property funds are higher up the risk scale than cash and fixed-interest bonds. Traditional property funds own a portfolio of properties which are rented out to tenants to provide you with a yield as well as capital appreciation if the value of the properties rises.

Property funds play a valuable role within a pension portfolio because property has a low correlation with shares. This means the two types of assets are influenced by different factors and often don't behave in the same way, which means your investment is more diversified.

Shares

Of the four assets types, shares are considered the riskiest because values can rise and fall very quickly. But they also have the greatest potential for capital growth over the long-term, which makes them a suitable asset for a pension (which often runs for several decades).

Traditionally, if there are still at least 10 years remaining before you retire, it would be suggested your pension be invested heavily in share-based funds to provide the maximum growth potential over the coming years.

Note:
However, due to the poor performance of the FTSE, other options need to be considered to achieve target growth. Be careful that your pension portfolio isn't too concentrated in any one area of investment. If you'd bought a technology fund just when the tech boom hit its peak in February, you'd have been pretty fed up two or even five years later. It's often argued that the easy option would be an index tracker fund.

An index tracker fund invests in all the companies quoted on a share index with the objective of mirroring - or 'tracking' - its performance. In other words, if you invest in a FTSE 100 tracker fund, your money will be invested in the top 100 U.K. companies. If they perform well, your investment will also rise in value (or depreciate accordingly).

So, that rounds up your main investment options. These days, it's a challenging time for pensions as all asset classes appear to be suffering. Bonds produced a negative return in 2006 while cash scraped in at less than 0.5%. Lately, the performance of U.K. shares has left a lot to be desired. And the property sector has definitely run out of steam for now. That said; try not to be too influenced by short-term returns. After all, pensions should be treated as a particularly long-term investment!

Your Quality Life Checklist

1. **Personal financial planning – Reduce your outgoings** ☐

2. **Asset build – Keep investments tangible and flexible** ☐

3. **Asset protection – Sort your wills and trusts** ☐

4. **Prepare for short or long term sickness – Lasting power of attorney** ☐

5. **Insurance – Explore the benefits and read the small print** ☐

6. **Prepare your family for life after your death** ☐

7. **Pension Planning – Traditional and/or SIPP to retire when you want to** ☐

8. **Biz - Online opportunities** ☐

9. **Business – Direct and MLM** ☐

10. **Plan investments to fit your short and long term needs** ☐

Additional Resources and Contacts

Books

Double Your Income Doing What You Love by Raymond Aaron www.UltimateAuthorBootcamp.com

Plan Now, Retire Happy: How to Secure Your Future, Whatever the Economic Climate: Planning Your Dream Retirement by Alvin Hall www.alvinhall.com

Brilliant Retirement: Your Practical Guide to a Happy, Healthy, Financially Sound Retirement by Dr Nic Peeling www.nicpeeling.com

Success Principles: How To Get From Where You Are To Where You Want To Be by Jack Canfield www.thesuccessprinciples.com

Websites

Annuities Online	www.Annuities-online.com
BBC online	www.bbc.co.uk
Investopedia	www.Investopedia.com
Money Marketing	www.Moneymarketing.com

Pension Calculator

Virgin Money	www.virginmoney.com
Aviva	www.aviva-pensioncalculator.co.uk
Money Advice Service	www.moneyadviceservice.co.uk

Government

Financial Services Authority (FSA)	www.fas.gov.uk
HM Revenue and Customs (HMRC)	www.hmrc.gov.uk

Newspapers

Daily Telegraph	www.telegraph.co.uk
Daily Mail	www.dailymail.co.uk
Daily Express	www.express.co.uk
Evening Standard	www.standard.co.uk
Financial Times	www.ft.com
FT Advisor	www.ftadvisor.com

Associate Partners

JMD Associates - Wills & Trusts	www.jmdassociates.co.uk
LJ Financial Planning – Financial Planning	www.ljfp.co.uk
Legacy Wealth Creation	www.legacywealthcreation.co.uk
Future In Safe Hands	www.futureinsafehands.com

Leading Business

PKM Associates	www.pkmgroup.co.uk

About the Authors

Pauline A Clarke

An established marketer and entrepreneur with over 20 years' experience in sales and marketing, Pauline has worked for known brands such as Carib Lager, Nourishment, Cockspur Rum and Dalgety Herbal Teas. A one-time restaurant owner, she branched out into consultancy assisting other restaurant owners, taking their business from where it is to where they want it to be. Most recently, Pauline developed awareness in finance and investments around pensions when she was provoked to look into her own situation. Prompted by Sean Freckleton of Legacy Wealth Creation, she learned about the current state of pensions and how to alleviate a poor retirement future by seeking out favourable investment options. Having shared her experience with close friends, she realised the information she acquired needed to be conveyed to ordinary people, helping them to make a difference for their own financial future. This experience is captured in *Wake Up, Smell The Money – 10 Steps to a Better Retirement Life*. Pauline can be contacted at pauline@pkmi.co.uk.

Kwame MA McPherson NC, HNC, CertMS, DipMS, MBA

A successful writer and Authorpreneur with many years experience in writing articles, short stories and fiction in numerous mediums, Kwame has also been on radio and television in various countries promoting his writing and the motivational work he does through his workshops. Kwame's experience is not dissimilar to Pauline's, where his attention was drawn to the dire state of his pension fund by two simple questions:

Do you know where your pension is?

Do you know its true value now and when you retire?

Alerted yet scared on the real status of his pension and his future retirement life, he decided he needed to take action – TODAY AND NOT TOMORROW. So armed with the new knowledge he obtained from experts in the field, like Sean Freckleton, he assessed his situation initiating steps to remedy an ever-decreasing fund and bleak future. His contribution to *Wake Up, Smell The Money – 10 Steps to a Better Retirement Life* is the result of his experience which he wishes to share with others who are facing an uncertain retirement future. Kwame can be contacted at: michael@pkmi.co.uk.

Index

Accounts-Receivable
   Financing 48
Alternative investments
   .... 39, 40
Alternative Investments
   .... 40, 41
annuity .. 30, 31, 32, 34,
   35, 36, 37, 38, 39, 49
Annuity 12, 36
annuity advice 31
Asset Protection Trusts
   47
assets 76
British Chambers of
   Commerce 23
Cash 79
Chancellor George
   Osborne 16
Chris Salith 21
Daily Express .. 15, 18, 23,
   87
Daily Mail 16, 22, 87
Daily Telegraph .. 12, See
   newspapers
David Kern 23
death 53
death benefit 51
Death insurance 53
deferring retirement .. 31
Direct revenue 64
early planning 25
Economy 23
Equity 49
Estate Planning 56
ETFs 76
Evening Standard .. 14, 15,
   87

exploring investment
   options 26
family limited partnership
   (FLP) 49
Family Limited
   Partnerships 49
Fixed Interest Bonds . 80
Form BR19 26
*Frozen To Death As Fuel
   Bills Soar* 16
Funded 61
Futures 76
Hedged funds 76
income protection 50
income-generating 18
Independent Financial
   Advisor 19, 29
Indirect revenue 65
investment 88
Investment Areas 75
Investment Planning . 73
investment strategy .. 28
Irrevocable 62
ISAs 27, 30, 80
Lasting Power of Attorney
   63
Life Insurance 51
Life Plan 51
Lisa A. Maini 68
Living Trust 60
Metro Newspaper 23
multi-level marketing 69
Old Age Care 15
Options 76
Origen 28
pension administrators .. 26
Pension Investments . 78
pension schemes 14, 38

Pension Tracing 26, 29
pension transfer values .26
premiums.....................55
Property 81
QNUPS........................44
Qualified Non-UK Resident Pension Scheme (QNUPS) 44
Referral marketing........65
Retirement 11, 86, 89
Revenue Streams 64
Revenue-producing assets......................19
revocable trust.............62
ROI.......................19, 42
SERP hotline 27
Shares.......................81
SIPP 28, 32, 38, 39, 40, 85
State of Retirement Report 14
stocks and shares.........75
term life insurance........54
Testamentary Trust 60
The Telegraph.co.uk 22
Tom Hopkins.................66
Trust 59
Trust Classifications ..60
Unfunded 61
Uniform Limited Partnership Act 49
Ways to Protect Assets 49
What Is An Annuity ...34
Will............................57
Wills 57

BONUSES

⭐ **FREE Pension Review**

⭐ **Your Investment Checklist**

⭐ **Seminar Pre-registration for upcoming PKM Group workshops and seminars**

⭐ **FREE tickets to upcoming LIFE CHANGING events**

Go to: www.pkmi.co.uk or email: info@pkmi.co.uk

NOTES

NOTES

NOTES

NOTES

NOTES

NOTES

NOTES

NOTES